NATURE WATCH

BUTTERFLIES

Written by
Sara Nelson

Lerner Publications Company • Minneapolis

Contents

Introducing the Butterfly	5
A Butterfly's Life Cycle	13
Butterfly Behaviors	25
Butterfly Enemies	33
Butterflies and People	37
Glossary	44
Selected Bibliography	45
Websites	46
Further Reading	46
Index	47

To Art Shapiro, my zoology advisor at UC Davis, who encouraged my study of writing and zoology and was kind enough to share his encyclopedic knowledge with a youngster.

Copyright © 2008 by Sara Nelson

All rights reserved. International copyright secured. No part of this book may be reproduced, stored in a retrieval system, or transmitted in any form or by any means—electronic, mechanical, photocopying, recording, or otherwise—without the prior written permission of Lerner Publishing Group, Inc., except for the inclusion of brief quotations in an acknowledged review.

Lerner Publications Company
A division of Lerner Publishing Group, Inc.
241 First Avenue North
Minneapolis, MN 55401

Website address: www.lernerbooks.com

Library of Congress Cataloging-in-Publication Data

Nelson, Sara Kirsten.
   Butterflies / by Sara Nelson.
     p. cm. — (Nature watch)
   Includes bibliographical references and index.
   ISBN-13: 978-0-8225-6766-0 (lib. bdg. : alk. paper)
   1. Butterflies—Juvenile literature. I. Title.
   QL544.2.N45 2008
   595.78'9—dc22   2006102792

Manufactured in the United States of America
1 2 3 4 5 6 – DP – 13 12 11 10 09 08

Above: Queen Alexandra's birdwing is one of the largest butterflies in the world. It is found in Papua New Guinea and the Solomon Islands. *Opposite:* An Indian leaf butterfly

Introducing the Butterfly

Walk through a flower garden in the summer, and you are likely to see butterflies. They flit from flower to flower, stopping now and then to take a drink of **nectar**.

There are about 24,000 different **species**, or kinds, of butterflies in the world. They come in all sizes. The largest butterfly is the white birdwing (also called Queen Alexandra's birdwing). This butterfly lives in the Solomon Islands of the western Pacific. It has a wingspan of 12 inches (30 cm). The dwarf blue butterflies that live in South Africa have a wingspan of only half an inch (1.3 cm).

Butterflies can live anywhere there are flowers. The only places on the planet they don't live are the ocean and the Antarctic. Most species of butterfly prefer only one or two types of **habitat**, but butterflies can be found in forests, grasslands, deserts, and mountains.

Butterflies live near rivers, fields, and sand dunes. They like open areas for sunbathing, with partly shady areas nearby so they can cool off. More butterflies live in the warm, humid tropics than anywhere else on the planet.

Butterflies are a kind of insect. They belong to an insect group, or order, called **Lepidoptera** (lep-uh-DOP-ter-uh).

Lepidoptera means "scaled winged," and the wings of butterflies are covered with tiny scales. Scientists think that butterflies appeared on Earth about 40 million years ago. Most insects in the Lepidoptera group feed on the nectar in flowers. Insects in this group go through four very different stages of development during their lives.

> No one is sure how butterflies got their name. Some think that they were named for the buttery color of the yellow brimstone butterfly. It is the first European butterfly to appear in the summer. Other people think that the name comes from fairy stories people used to tell. A long time ago, some people thought that witches turned into butterflies and stole milk and butter from farms. That might be why we call these insects butterflies.

Right: A privet hawk moth clings to a tree trunk. Moths also belong to the order Lepidoptera. Moths fold their wings when resting, while butterflies hold their wings together straight up above their backs.

Above: A giant swallowtail butterfly rests on a zinnia. From the side, it's easy to see its two different sets of wings. *Inset:* The small copper butterfly has long antennae.

BUTTERFLY BODIES

Like all insects, butterflies have an **exoskeleton**. This means the outside layers of their bodies are covered with a stiff material called **chiton**. Like other insects, butterfly bodies are divided into three parts. They are the head, the **thorax**, and the **abdomen**. The thorax, or middle part of the butterfly's body, has two pairs of wings and three pairs of legs. A butterfly has two **forewings** and two hindwings that are linked together. Linked wings make it easier to fly. **Antennae**, or long, skinny feelers, are on top of their heads.

Above: Like all butterflies, this male arota copper butterfly has a pair of short front legs.
Lower left: A special photograph, called a micrograph, shows a monarch butterfly's claw. Claws help butterflies hold on to flowers or other sources of food.
Upper left: A female orange tip butterfly walks on its four long legs.

The chiton that covers the three parts of a butterfly's body is hard and waterproof. It has flexible plates at the joints between parts. Butterflies have six long, slender, jointed legs. Four of the butterfly's legs have claws so the insect can perch safely. They use the two tiny legs in front to groom themselves. They can walk on their four big legs, but they prefer to fly.

Butterflies have huge eyes. Each eye is made up of thousands of little lenses that work together to build a complete picture. For this reason, they are called compound eyes. Some butterflies have 20,000 lenses in each eye! Scientists still don't know exactly what butterflies can see, but they think they can see color and movement. Scientists do know that butterflies can see **ultraviolet light**, a kind of light that is invisible to humans.

A butterfly's antennae can pick up smells and send this information to the brain. The brain recognizes the different perfumes of the flowers it feeds on. The antennae can also pick up sounds and gauge wind speed.

A painted lady butterfly's eye *(center right)*

The butterfly has **palps**, or feelers, near its mouth. It uses its palps to smell and to taste. It can also taste with the hairs on its feet. It gathers food with a long, hollow tubelike organ called a **proboscis** (pro-BOSS-kiss). It uses this tube to suck nectar from flowers. Depending on the size of the butterfly, the proboscis can be a fraction of an inch or more than 1-foot (30 cm) long. When a butterfly isn't eating, the proboscis stays curled up just outside its mouth.

Butterflies taste with the hairs on their feet. Their feet can sense if they are near food. A butterfly will uncurl its proboscis to drink if it is placed standing in sugar water. But it won't do this if it stands in plain water.

The tubelike tongue, or proboscis, of this nocturne butterfly curls up toward its mouth.

Above: A close-up image shows the rows of scales on a giant swallowtail butterfly's wing.
Right: The colorful scales on a birdwing swallowtail butterfly's wing overlap like shingles on a roof.

All butterflies have color on their wings. Some have different colors depending on whether they are male or female. Some of the scales on the wings contain color. Other scales reflect light in certain ways which gives them color. The ridges on some scales reflect light in such a way as to give the wings a shiny look.

The butterfly has a long, hollow heart that runs through its entire abdomen. Muscles in the heart pump blood freely through the body. Butterfly blood is usually clear, yellow, or green in color. The veins in a butterfly's wings give them extra support and strength, though a little bit of blood flows through them as well.

Butterflies breathe by taking in air through holes in their thorax and abdomen. These tubes carry oxygen to all parts of the butterfly body. The insect releases waste gases through those same holes.

A butterfly's stomach consists of a series of chambers that run in a long tube just below the heart from the mouth and along the abdomen. The stomach processes food to give the butterfly energy to live. Food wastes pass out through the anus.

Warming Up

Butterfly bodies have no way of heating themselves—or cooling down. This means that their bodies are the same temperature as the air surrounding them. They have to wait for the sun to warm them. Early in the morning, the cool butterfly is likely to be sitting still. As the sun warms the morning air, the butterfly will open its wings. The blood in the wing veins also helps to warm the butterfly as it sunbathes. Once it is completely warmed up, it will be able to fly away in search of food.

Butterflies living in cold climates often have dark wings or dark patches. This dark coloring is better at capturing heat. The lighter colors and ridges on the scales of tropical butterflies cause light and heat to bounce off their wings. The light markings help the butterflies stay cool. Other butterflies may be lighter or darker according to the season of the year. This way, these butterflies can keep from becoming too cold or too hot.

Some butterflies living in places that are very cold, windy, or dry have other traits that help them survive. Butterflies that live high up in the mountains, for instance, are smaller than most other butterflies. Being smaller, they have smaller wings and bodies, so they lose heat more slowly. Their small size also allows them to hide easily so they are not blown away by strong mountain winds.

The light coloring of a great southern white butterfly helps it stay cool in its home in Everglades National Park in Florida.

A Butterfly's Life Cycle

During its lifetime, a butterfly goes through four stages: egg *(above)*, **larva**, **pupa**, and adult. The butterfly looks and behaves very differently at each of these stages. This process of changing forms is called **metamorphosis**.

The butterfly begins its life as an egg. Like most animals, male butterflies make sperm and female butterflies create eggs. When these combine inside the female butterfly, she is able to lay eggs that will eventually turn into new butterflies.

Depending on the species, a single butterfly can lay anywhere from twenty to more than a thousand eggs. The more eggs a butterfly lays, the better its chances that at least some of them will hatch and survive to become adults. Eggs vary in size, but most are very small with a soft, leathery shell. They are usually yellow or green and darken as they get close to hatching.

A female map butterfly lays sticky stacks of eggs underneath a nettle leaf.

Some butterflies lay one egg at a time, while others lay them in large batches. But some butterflies scatter their eggs as they fly. Although butterflies abandon their eggs and let their young fend for themselves, some females lay their eggs on the protected underside of leaves. This way, the eggs are shaded so they don't get too hot or dry. They are also hidden from birds and other animals that might eat them.

LARVAE

Caterpillars, called larvae, develop inside the eggs. The yolk inside the egg feeds the growing larva. The caterpillars will hatch, depending on the kind, anytime from a few days to more than a month after the eggs have been laid. The eggshell becomes its first real meal after it hatches. Then the caterpillar's job is to eat until it grows to its full size. While some butterfly larvae aren't choosy about what they eat, others stick with only one kind of plant. Some eat flowers, leaves, or buds, while others eat insects—ant larvae or aphids, for example—or even other caterpillars. Roots, stems, or stored grain make a tasty meal for some species. Most butterflies lay their eggs on plants that the newly hatched caterpillars will eat. That way, the caterpillars will have food ready and waiting for them.

Right: Map butterfly larvae begin to hatch from their eggs.
Below: A butterfly larva eats its eggshell.

Cabbage white butterfly caterpillars like broccoli.

Peacock butterflies live in Europe and eat nettles during their caterpillar stage. Cabbage white caterpillars eat only plants belonging to the cabbage family. These plants have certain oils that other insects don't like the taste of. As a result, the peacock and cabbage white caterpillars have these plants all to themselves.

The blue butterfly caterpillar has a gland in its back that produces a sweet liquid. Ants like it so much they bring the larva back to the ant nest, and the caterpillar eats ant larvae while the ants eat the liquid.

Caterpillars eat so much that they outgrow their skin. They have to shed their old skin in a process called **molting**. When this happens, the caterpillar stops eating. It produces a sticky liquid from an organ beneath its mouth called a spinneret. The liquid hardens into a sticky thread, and the caterpillar uses this thread to attach itself to a leaf or twig. As the caterpillar hangs there, its skin splits open along the back. The larva crawls out, wearing its new baggy skin, which stretches easily. As the caterpillar eats and grows, the skin becomes smoother and tighter. Then the caterpillar has to molt again. Most butterfly larvae molt four or five times.

A hungry question mark butterfly caterpillar is chewing apart the leaves of a hops vine.

Caterpillars look nothing like the butterflies they will become—even after molting. Their eyes are simpler than those of the adult butterfly, and they lack wings, proboscis, and reproductive organs. Instead of the proboscis, caterpillars have strong jaws for chewing. Their bodies have thirteen segments and eight pairs of legs. Three pairs of legs have claws, four pairs have small hooks, and one pair, called prolegs, have suckers at the end. Waves of muscle action throughout a caterpillar's body help move its legs. And all those legs carry the caterpillar around in search of food.

The mourning cloak butterfly caterpillar is spiny.

Three clawed legs of this Old World swallowtail butterfly caterpillar are visible in this photo.

Some caterpillars are smooth, and some are hairy. Some have spines. Certain species have hairs that cause stinging or itching so that other animals think twice about eating them. Some caterpillars contain poisons that they make from the plants they eat. These poisons can make their enemies sick or even kill them. Many poisonous caterpillars are brightly colored to warn off animals that might want to eat them.

THE CHRYSALIS

When a caterpillar has reached full size, it creates a button of silk on a leaf or twig. Then it hangs, usually head down, from this button. Some caterpillars add a silk sash around their middles for extra support. The larva molts again, but this time, the caterpillar's new skin is a **chrysalis** (KRIH-suh-lis). The chrysalis is hard and sometimes thorny. Sometimes it looks like a leaf or twig. Inside, the caterpillar has become a pupa. The chrysalis protects the pupa, which can't move or defend itself in any way.

The chrysalis hangs in place for a few days to six months, depending on the species. The pupa inside it turns to a soupy liquid. In this soup, wings, legs, compound eyes, and antennae form. Reproductive organs mature. Although the chrysalis looks the same from the outside, a butterfly has grown inside.

Left: A monarch butterfly caterpillar begins forming its chrysalis.
Below: This chrysalis has a silk thread to help support it on the branch. From it, a black swallowtail butterfly will emerge.

When the new butterfly is ready to come out, it pumps body fluids into its head and thorax to make them swell. This helps the butterfly break through the hard shell of the chrysalis that has protected it. Pushing with its legs, the butterfly climbs free. It is not yet ready to fly away, however. Its body needs to expand and harden. Its wings are wet and crumpled. They need to dry in the sun. The butterfly pumps blood into the wings to fill them out. The whole process takes 10 to 20 minutes. Then the butterfly flies to the nearest flower or other food source.

If a new butterfly isn't able to expand its body and wings quickly, it will be crippled for life.

Above: A small tortoiseshell butterfly leaves its chrysalis.
Below: A question mark butterfly steps away from its chrysalis and stretches its wings.

A mourning cloak butterfly rests on an aster. A male of this species seeking a mate will chase other males out of its territory.

THE BUTTERFLY

Just as the caterpillar's task is to eat, the adult butterfly's task is to mate. To mate, males and females must find one another. Some males, like mourning cloak butterflies, stake out territories. They chase other males away while they wait for females to fly by. The males of Central and South American cracker butterflies make sharp snapping sounds with their wings as they fight with male rivals in the air. Some male butterflies lie in wait for a female as she develops inside her chrysalis. A few species even mate with the female before she emerges.

Red admiral butterflies land close to each other on an oak tree. They may be preparing to mate.

Most butterflies choose their mate using sight and smell. They recognize one another by color, by wing shape, and by flight pattern. Males and females of some species look very different from one another, but in other species they are very much alike. African white butterflies show color differences between the sexes that humans can't detect. The patterns on their wings only show as ultraviolet light.

Scent is even more important in helping butterflies find a mate. The males produce a scent from glands on wings, legs, and abdomen that attracts females. These scents are called **pheromones** (FARE-uh-mones). The males of many kinds of butterflies dust the female with scent particles. This is usually done to make the female want to mate, but in some kinds of butterflies, this scent scares away rival males.

During a courtship dance, mating butterflies explore each other with their antennae. The two butterflies fly in patterns around each other. This shows off their wings and sends their scent toward each other. Eventually, the two butterflies join abdomens, and the male passes a package of sperm to the female. Butterflies mate once. The female stores the sperm until she has found a good spot to deposit the eggs.

A butterfly can live for a few weeks to a year, depending on the species. But males die soon after mating and females soon after laying eggs. The eggs are the beginning of a new generation. They will hatch into caterpillars, undergo metamorphosis, and continue the cycle.

Metamorphosis gives the insect some advantages that other animals don't have. Each form has its own task, so the butterfly doesn't need to spend energy developing body parts it doesn't need. The caterpillar, for instance, doesn't need the organs or senses used in mating. Instead, it is able to spend time and energy on eating and growing. The adult butterfly concentrates on mating and laying eggs to create the new generation.

Silver-studded blue butterflies mate on a flower.

Above: Clearwing butterflies drink nectar from many angles.
Opposite: A cabbage white butterfly draws nectar from an orange flower.

Butterfly Behaviors

Butterflies find food using sight, smell (using their antennae), and taste (using their hairy feet). They tend to feed from brightly colored flowers, especially those that are orange, red, or deep pink. Some butterflies have a very long proboscis perfect for reaching nectar at the very bottom of a long, tubular flower. Other species have a short proboscis. These butterflies feed from flowers with short, wide blossoms. This way, the butterflies don't compete for the same food.

Many butterflies feed from a number of different kinds of plants. They usually only sip from one kind at a time, though. When that flower stops blooming, the butterfly moves on to another kind.

When butterflies sip nectar from a flower, they brush up against the flower's pollen, the powdery part of the blossom. Then they fly away with some pollen on their bodies. When they go to the next blossom, some of that pollen comes off. Most flowers need pollen from another flower to make seeds. By carrying pollen from blossom to blossom, butterflies help flowers to reproduce. Since they visit only one kind of flower at a time, butterflies better **pollinate** each kind. Butterflies and moths are the fourth most important insect pollinators, after bees, ants, and wasps.

OTHER BUTTERFLY FOODS
Instead of drinking flower nectar, longwing butterflies eat pollen. The pollen has more food value than nectar, so longwings live longer and reproduce more often than most other butterflies.

Right: This tiger longwing butterfly is ready to eat the pollen on its proboscis.
Below: A longwing butterfly shows off the length of its wings.

Some kinds of butterflies—like the brown hairstreak butterfly—eat a sweet liquid that is given off by aphids. These kinds of insects suck the sap from plants. The sap has so much sugar that the aphid can't digest it all. It leaves some behind as waste. This waste is called honeydew. The butterflies feed on this honeydew.

Some butterflies, such as mourning cloaks, feed on sap from trees or vines. Red admiral butterflies enjoy sap too, but they also eat rotten fruit. Males of certain species, such as tiger swallowtail butterflies, get salts they need from mud puddles. Some butterflies may get their vitamins and minerals from dead animals or animal dung. Butterflies sometimes land on people to suck their sweat on a hot day!

Right: **Butterflies don't just land on humans to rest. Some of them drink our sweat.**
Below: **Male yellow butterflies suck minerals from dung.**

Mourning cloak butterflies live near wooded waterways because their caterpillars eat tree sap.

Butterflies usually live near the kinds of food their caterpillars eat. For instance, the caterpillars of the mourning cloak butterfly eat sap from willow, elm, birch, and poplar trees. These trees usually grow near sources of water. Mourning cloak butterflies live near woodland rivers, streams, and ponds in Europe and North America.

Butterflies in Winter

Since insects can't control their body temperature, they can't be active when it is cold. Those that feed on nectar are not able to find flowers in the winter, either. A few kinds of butterflies **migrate**, or fly, to warmer climates to escape the cold. Cabbage butterflies travel for 12 hours at a stretch and can cover 250 miles (400 km) in three days. Red admirals migrate south after they lay their eggs. They often fly in small groups, but some migrate with other species of butterflies, bees, and even migrating birds.

Monarch butterflies are the most famous migrating butterflies in North America. During the summer, they live throughout the United States and Canada.

In the fall, monarchs fly to central Mexico, Florida, or the California coast. During these migrations, the butterflies travel 2,000 miles (3,220 km) or more. Monarchs travel in large numbers, and thousands of them spend the winter on certain trees in Mexico every year. Sometimes these butterflies cover the entire tree!

Although a single monarch butterfly will travel south to Mexico or California, one butterfly does not make the entire journey north. Instead, monarchs produce

Monarch butterflies crowd together on a tree trunk in Mexico.

several generations while migrating north. They mate in the spring as they fly, laying their eggs as they go. When these eggs have hatched and changed from caterpillars to adult butterflies, these new butterflies continue the flight north. Sometimes migrating monarchs have been blown off course and landed in Britain, Hawaii, and even China. Monarchs can't live and reproduce in Europe, Hawaii, or Asia, because they feed on the milkweed plants, which don't grow in most of those regions.

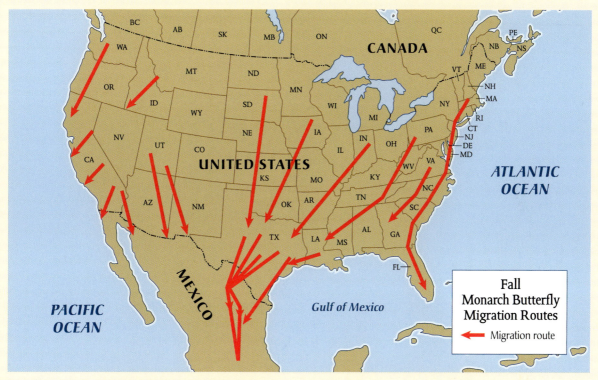

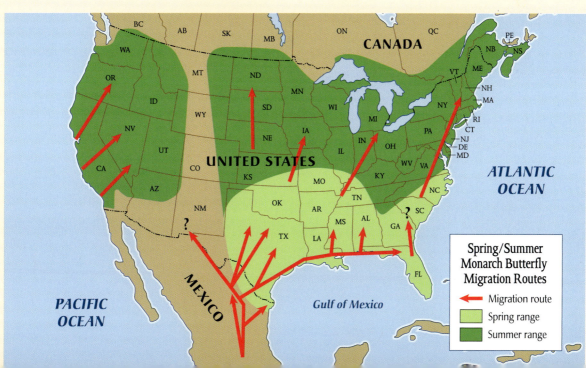

The comma butterfly hibernates in the winter.

Other butterflies **hibernate**. Their bodies shut down until the weather has turned warmer. Different species of butterflies hibernate at different stages in their life cycles. Some hibernate as eggs or caterpillars, while others hibernate as pupae or adults. Normal body functions slow down in hibernating butterflies. When this happens, the butterflies don't need food or warmth. They can just sit tight until winter is over or conditions improve. Some hibernating butterflies can withstand temperatures of -20°F (-29°C) or lower.

Peacock butterflies hibernate as adults. The leaflike pattern on the undersides of their wings helps them hide from predators. Mourning cloak butterflies hibernate folded up underneath leaves. Comma and small tortoiseshell butterflies also hibernate during the winter. Commas crawl to the underside of leaves and close their wings so that they look like dead leaves. In the fall, this butterfly produces new chemicals in its blood that act like anti-freeze. In the spring, the butterfly stops producing these chemicals. Scientists think perhaps the changes in the amount of daylight trigger the amount of chemical the butterfly produces.

Peacock butterflies hibernate for 5 to 6 months during the winter. Females lay eggs in the spring.

Above: A golden silk spider attacks a butterfly caught in its web.
Opposite: A white-fronted bee-eater has captured a painted lady butterfly.

Butterfly Enemies

Birds, bats, lizards, spiders, wasps, dragonflies, and praying mantises find butterflies a tasty treat. They are **predators**, animals that eat other animals. In fact, butterflies can be eaten at any phase of their life cycle. Beetles and lacewings eat butterfly eggs. So do snails. Frogs and toads will eat both caterpillars and butterflies.

Butterflies face many predators, but they also have many ways to escape being eaten. Their good eyesight and flying ability help them. Grayling butterflies fly toward the sun to escape predators. Looking into the sun, the predator has a hard time seeing the fleeing butterfly.

Mourning cloak butterflies play dead. Predators that attack only moving **prey** ignore them. Red admiral caterpillars protect themselves by joining nettle leaves together to make a shelter. Most predators won't risk getting stung by the nettles and leave the caterpillars alone.

Above: From any angle, a dead leaf butterfly can hide in plain sight. Both its forewings and its hindwings look like leaves. *Right:* A variable cracker butterfly's wings combine dark spots that look like tree bark and light spots that look like moss or fungus.

Some caterpillars will drop off a leaf, falling to the ground to escape. Caterpillars of brown butterflies feed at night. Most butterfly predators hunt only during the day, so they miss these caterpillars. Some caterpillars, like the swallowtails, smell bad. Postman butterflies don't taste good, so predators avoid them. Mourning cloak caterpillars vibrate, and this scares many predators away.

Other kinds of butterflies have colors and shapes that help them blend into their surroundings so that predators don't see them. The dead leaf butterfly, for instance, looks like a dead leaf. Birds don't see the color blue very well, so blue butterflies don't attract their attention. Some butterflies and caterpillars look like twigs. Swallowtail butterfly caterpillars look like bird droppings.

FOOLING THE ENEMY

Some kinds of butterflies don't blend in at all. They have colors or patterns on the wings that surprise, confuse, or frighten predators. Long tails, such as the tails of metalmark butterflies, or big **eyespots** on wings of satyr and wood nymph butterflies help keep them safe. Birds tend to peck at these eyespots and not at the butterfly's body. Sometimes the eyespots or long tail make the predator think the butterfly is bigger than it is. Some caterpillars also have eyespots.

A butterfly's color can also warn off predators. Certain colors are signs of danger in the insect world. Bees, for instance, have black and yellow stripes. Bees are likely to sting, so predators tend to avoid any insect with black and yellow markings. The same holds true for red and black or orange and black. The monarch butterfly's orange and black wings warn off enemies.

Monarch caterpillars eat milkweed, and milkweed contains a poison. The poison stays in the monarch's body when it becomes a butterfly. Predators quickly learn not to eat these butterflies. Birthwort butterflies, sweet oil butterflies, and swallowtail butterflies all eat poisonous plants and advertise it in their coloring.

Right: A spicebush swallowtail caterpillar hides in a spicebush leaf tube. Only its eyespots show.
Below: A metalmark butterfly has more than one trick to fool predators. It has long hindwings that make it look bigger than it really is. But it also has blue coloring, which is hard for birds to see.

Some nonpoisonous butterflies look like the poisonous ones. For example, the viceroy butterfly is tasty, but it looks so much like a monarch that predators leave it alone. These butterflies use **mimicry**. This means they have the same patterns or colors as the poisonous or bad-tasting butterflies. Some of these mimics are poisonous themselves. This way, the predator gets a double warning of the butterfly's danger and learns more quickly.

Which one is the monarch butterfly, and which one is the viceroy? If you were a hungry predator, would you take a chance at guessing wrong? The answer is on page 46.

Butterflies and People

FARMERS SOMETIMES CONSIDER BUTTERFLIES PESTS. Though butterflies often help plants by pollinating them, some caterpillars eat plants. Swallowtail larvae eat citrus leaves, so people who grow oranges and lemons don't like to have these butterflies around. Cabbage butterfly caterpillars eat cabbage, broccoli, and other plants of the cabbage family. Farmers growing plants of this family consider these butterflies serious pests. One way gardeners and farmers limit the damage done by cabbage butterflies is to release certain kinds of wasps in the area. These wasps lay their eggs on the cabbage butterfly caterpillars. When the wasp larvae hatch, they eat the caterpillar.

On the other hand, painted lady caterpillars can be considered helpful insects. They eat enough thistle plants to help keep these weeds from overrunning farmland.

Although butterflies can avoid or escape many predators, they have no way of fooling human beings. Butterflies are in danger from human activities. Humans use poisons to kill insect pests, and many of these poisons kill butterflies too. People also clear land for building and, in doing so, destroy places where butterflies rest, lay eggs, or feed. Farming, ranching, logging, and construction projects all destroy butterfly habitat.

Many butterflies only eat from one kind of flower. Once that flower's habitat disappears, the butterflies that rely on it are gone too. As large numbers of a butterfly species die, it becomes harder for remaining butterflies to find mates. A butterfly is considered **threatened** when the total numbers of its kind are low. Butterflies with even fewer numbers are **endangered**. Once a butterfly is **extinct**, it is gone forever.

Left: The Karner blue butterfly is an endangered species.
Below: Clearing land for buildings destroys butterfly habitats.

A Schaus's swallowtail butterfly

A beautiful blue butterfly called the xerces blue once lived in California. It became extinct in 1943. A number of butterflies related to it are in danger of disappearing too. Because so many people have moved to California, houses and shopping malls have destroyed the butterflies' habitats. The largest remaining patch of land available for the El Segundo blue butterfly belongs to the Los Angeles airport.

California butterflies are not the only ones in trouble. The Oregon silverspot became endangered as houses swallowed up its habitat. Coastal development and mosquito poison threaten Schaus's swallowtail butterflies. Butterflies that live in the tropical rain forests are in danger because the forests are being cleared for farming and logging.

The largest butterfly in the world, Queen Alexandra's birdwing, is endangered because of logging and the clearing of land to grow palm oil trees in Papua New Guinea. Even monarchs are struggling. Construction is destroying their breeding grounds, and their food, milkweed, has been pulled up by people weeding their gardens.

> In Africa and in Mexico, certain kinds of caterpillars are a delicious snack for humans.

Swallowtail butterflies lick salt from a mud puddle in Argentina. Some countries in which swallowtails are rare, such as Britain, protect them.

In 2007, the government of Taiwan, an island off the southeast coast of Asia, sealed off 600 yards (550 m) of a highway to protect migrating purple milkweed butterflies. These butterflies, like the monarchs of North America, feed on milkweed plants as caterpillars. They migrate 180 miles (290 km) from the northern part of the island to the southern part to escape winter cold. The butterflies rest on warm pavement at night, where cars can crush them. Nets along the highway and ultraviolet lights on an overpass help them cross the road safely.

People to the Rescue

Many conservation organizations work to make sure that wild lands are saved so they can serve as habitats for many kinds of wildlife. Parks and national wetlands protect woods, meadows, and marshes where butterflies live. Swallowtail butterflies are protected by law in Britain and other countries. In 2000, the president of Mexico created a reserve for wintering monarch butterflies in that country.

Many people from all over the world travel to Mexico to see the huge numbers of monarch butterflies that have migrated to certain areas of that country. These tourists buy food and stay in hotels, which brings jobs to the people in those areas.

The Butterfly Conservation Initiative organizes many butterfly protection groups so that they work together. One of these groups, the Xerces Society, was named after the extinct butterfly, but it protects many different kinds of animals. Monarch Watch teaches people about the migration of monarch butterflies and the difficulties they face.

Scientists in the Mexican state of Michoacán gather monarch butterflies to study.

Above: On a butterfly farm, visitors may see several stages of butterflies' life cycle in one area.
Opposite: A boy uses a magnifying glass to help him identify a butterfly.

In some tropical countries like Papua New Guinea and Costa Rica, people farm butterflies, raising them for collectors and butterfly exhibits. Butterfly farming pays enough money to feed and clothe farmers' families so that they don't have to destroy forests to create land on which to raise crops.

All of us can plant a variety of the flowers that butterflies like. If we all work to protect butterflies and make sure that their habitats are preserved, the butterflies will survive. We can also share our knowledge of butterflies with others. We can tell them about butterfly eyes. We can explain that butterflies taste with their feet. We can watch a caterpillar make a chrysalis and turn into a butterfly. We can enjoy butterflies as they pollinate the flowers in our garden, and we can marvel at the tricks they use to escape from predators. We can teach others how to protect butterfly habitats so that butterflies are always around to delight human beings.

GLOSSARY

abdomen: the hindmost section of an insect that contains an insect's heart, stomach, and reproductive organs

antennae: the feelers on a butterfly's head

chiton: a hard, waterproof outer skeleton

chrysalis: a hard covering that protects the pupa as it turns into an adult butterfly

endangered: likely to die out or become extinct unless steps are taken to prevent extinction

exoskeleton: the hard outer covering that makes up an insect's skeleton

extinct: when there are no more members of a particular species

eyespots: markings that look like large eyes, used to frighten predators

forewings: the large set of wings in front of a smaller pair

habitat: a place where an animal lives

hibernate: a process of shutting down bodily systems in order to survive cold or lack of food

larva: an immature insect; a caterpillar is a butterfly larva

Lepidoptera: the order of insects to which butterflies and moths belong

metamorphosis: a process of radical change; the transition from egg to caterpillar to pupa to butterfly is called complete metamorphosis

migrate: to move from one place in order to settle in another

mimicry: copying another animal's appearance

molting: the shedding of old skin or feathers during growth

nectar: the sweet liquid produced by some flowers

palps: small feelers near an insect's mouth

pheromones: chemical signals detected by a sense of smell

pollinate: to carry pollen from one flower to another, enabling that second flower to produce seeds

predators: animals that kill and eat other animals to survive

prey: animals that are eaten by other animals

proboscis: a long, hollow tubelike tongue

pupa: the stage between the larva and the adult in some insects

species: a kind of animal or plant

thorax: the middle part of a butterfly's body, where the wings and legs are attached

threatened: in danger of dying out or becoming endangered or extinct

ultraviolet light: light with a wavelength that humans can't see, but butterflies can

SELECTED BIBLIOGRAPHY

American Museum of Natural History. "A Curious Cash Crop: Butterflies." *American Museum of Natural History.* N.d. http://sciencebulletins.amnh.org/biobulletin/biobulletin/story876.html (June 19, 2007).

Ayto, John. *Arcade Dictionary of Word Origins.* New York: Arcade Publishing, 1990.

Burton, Maurice. *The Life of Insects.* New York: Golden Press, 1972.

The Butterfly Conservation Initiative. "Butterfly Resources." *BFCI.* 2006. http://www.butterflyrecovery.org (June 15, 2007).

Hutchinson, Peter, ed. *How Insects Live.* New York: Phaidon, 1976.

Johnson, Willis H., Louis E. Delanney, Eliot C. Williams, and Thomas Cole. *Principles of Zoology.* New York: Holt, Rinehart and Winston, 1969.

Klots, Alexander B., and Elsie B. Klots. *Living Insects of the World.* Garden City, NY: Doubleday and Company, 1975.

LaFleur, Donna. "An Enchantment of Butterflies: Tips for Beginning Butterfly Gardeners." *Louisiana Public Broadcasting.* N.d. http://www.lpb.org/programs/butterflies/gardening.html (June 19, 2007).

Lepidopterists' Society. "The Butterfly and Moth FAQ Page." *Lepidopterists' Society.* N.d. http://www.lepsoc.org (June 15, 2007).

Moure, Orlando. "Protection for Monarch Butterfly: A Decree from Mexican President." *OM Personal Home Page.* N.d. http://www.ompersonal.com.ar/ecology/monarchbutterflyprotection.htm (June 15, 2007).

MSN. "Butterflies and Moths." *Encarta.* 2007. http:/encarta.msn.com/encyclopedia_761578331/Butterflies_and_Moths.html (June 15, 2007).

New Hampshire Public Television. "Zebra Longwing Butterfly: Heliconius charitonius." *Nature Watch.* 2007. http://www.nhptv.org/Natureworks/zebralongwing.htm (June 15, 2007).

North American Butterfly Association. "Butterfly Questions and Answers." *NABA.* January 15, 2007. http://www.naba.org (June 15, 2007).

Ramel, Gordon. "Gordon's Aphid Page." *Earth-Life.* February 27, 2007. http://www.earthlife.net/insects/aphids.html (June 15, 2007).

University of Kentucky Department of Entomology. "Butterfly Gardens." *University of Kentucky.* 2007. http://www.uky.edu/Ag/Entomology (June 15, 2007).

Virginia Technical Institute. "Aphids." Virginia Cooperative Extension. N.d. http://www.ext.vt.edu/departments/entomology/ornamentals/aphids.html (June 15, 2007).

Xerces Society. "California Monarch Butterfly Conservation Campaign." *Xerces Society.* 2007. http://www.xerces.org/Monarch_Butterfly_Conservation/index.htm (June 15, 2007).

WEBSITES

Enchanted Learning. "Queen Alexandra's Birdwing Butterfly"
http://www.enchantedlearning.com/subjects/butterfly/species/Queenalex.shtml.
Learn more about the Queen Alexandra's birdwing butterfly on this website.

Koday, Ed. "Koday's Kids: Amazing Insects"
http://www.ivyhall.district96.k12.il.us/4TH/KKHP/1INSECTS/bugmenu.html.
This website contains pictures of insects, from the dragonfly to the assassin bug.

Smithsonian Institution, Department of Systematic Biology, Entomology Section, National Museum of Natural History. "Bug Info: The Most Incredible Insects"
http://www.si.edu/resource/faq/nmnh/buginfo/incredbugs/butterfliesus.htm. Explore the Smithsonian Institution website to discover more incredible insects and butterflies.

FURTHER READING

Latimer, Jonathan P., Karen S. Nolting, and Virginia Marie Peterson. *Young Naturalist Guide to Butterflies*. Boston: Houghton Mifflin, 2000.

Latimer, Jonathan P., and Karen S. Nolting. *Young Naturalist Guide to Caterpillars*. Boston: Houghton Mifflin, 2000.

Pringle, Laurence. *An Extraordinary Life: The Story of a Monarch Butterfly*. New York: Orchard Books, 1997.

Stewart, Melissa. *A Place for Butterflies*. Atlanta, GA: Peachtree Publishers, 2006.

Waxman, Laura Hamilton. *Monarch Butterflies*. Minneapolis, MN: Lerner Publications Company, 2003.

Whalley, Paul. *Eyewitness: Butterfly and Moth*. New York: DK Children, 2000.

Zemlicka, Shannon. *From Egg to Butterfly*. Minneapolis: Lerner Publications Company, 2003.

Answer to quiz on page 36: The butterfly on the left is the monarch.

INDEX

ant larvae, 15

body, 42; abdomen, 7, 22; antennae, 7, 9, 19, 22, 25; body temperature, 12, 28, 30; chiton, 7–8; claws, 8, 18; compound eyes, 9, 16, 19; exoskeleton, 7; forewings, 7, 34; heart, 11; hindwings, 7, 34; legs, 7–8, 19–20, 22; palps, 10; proboscis, 10, 18, 25–26; prolegs, 18; scales, 6, 11; spinneret, 17; stomach, 11; thorax, 7, 20
Butterfly Conservation Initiative, 41
butterfly farms, 42

cabbage white butterfly, 24–25, 28; caterpillars, 37; larvae, 16
caterpillar, 15–18, 23, 33–34, 37, 40
chrysalis, 19–21

eating, 5–6, 10, 15, 16–18, 20–21, 23–28, 37; aphids, 15, 27; cabbage, 37; citrus, 37; broccoli, 16, 37; honeydew, 27; hops, 17; milkweed, 29, 35, 39–40; nectar, 5–6, 10, 24–25, 28; pollen, 25–26; puddling, 27; thistle, 37
eggs. *See* life cycle
endangered, 38; Karner blue butterfly, 38
extinction, 38; xerces blue butterfly, 39

habitats, 5, 38–42
hibernate, 30

Indian leaf butterfly, 4–5

Lepidoptera, 6
life cycle, 13, 3, 33; egg, 13–15, 22–23, 28; larva, 13, 15–17; pupa, 13, 19; adult, 13, 21–23, 28

map butterfly, 14; larvae, 15
mating, 21–23, 26; pheromones, 22

metamorphosis, 13, 23
micrograph, 8
migrate, 28–29, 40–41
milk thief (milchdieb), 6
molting, 17
monarch butterfly, 8, 28–29, 36, 39, 41; caterpillar, 19; larva, 15; Monarch Watch, 41; reserve, 40
moths, 6, 26
mourning cloak butterfly, 20, 27–28, 30, 33–34; caterpillar, 18

painted lady butterfly, 9, 32–33
peacock butterfly, 16, 30–31
predators, 33–36, 38, 42
protection, 33–36; camouflage, 34; coloring, 34; eyespots, 35; mimicry, 36; playing dead, 33–37; poison, 18, 35–36

Queen Alexandra's birdwing, 4, 39; wingspan, 5
question mark butterfly, 20; caterpillar, 17

red admiral butterfly, 22, 27–28, 33

silk, 19
small tortoiseshell butterfly, 20, 30
species, 5, 15, 19, 21–23
swallowtail butterfly, 7, 11, 19, 27, 35, 39–40; larvae, 37

threatened, 38

ultraviolet light, 9, 22

white birdwing, *See* Queen Alexandra's birdwing

Xerces Society, 41

ABOUT THE AUTHOR

Sara Nelson was born in Minnesota and grew up in Southern California. She received her undergraduate degree in English and Zoology from the University of California at Davis. After that she spent two years in St. Andrews, Scotland, and received her MFA in poetry from Washington University in St. Louis.

Sara returned to Minnesota where she has taught English and other subjects to junior and senior high students at Montessori schools in the area.

PHOTO ACKNOWLEDGEMENTS

The images in this book are used with the permission of: PhotoDisc Royalty Free by Getty Images, all backgrounds, pp. 1, 5, 13, 25, 33, 37, 38 (bottom), 44-48; © Dorling Kindersley/Dave King/Getty Images, pp. 2-3; © Francois Gilson/Peter Arnold, Inc., p. 4; © R. Al Simpson/Visuals Unlimited, p. 5; © age fotostock/SuperStock, pp. 6, 10, 18 (left), 33, 34 (left); © Richard Day/Daybreak Imagery, pp. 7 (main), 13, 17, 19 (left), 20 (bottom), 21, 35 (right), 36 (both); © Wim Van Egmond/Visuals Unlimited, p. 7 (inset); © Adrian Davies/naturepl.com, p. 8 (upper left); © Dennis Kunkel/Oxford Scientific Films, p. 8 (lower left); © Steve Graser/Visuals Unlimited, pp. 8 (right), 9; © John Gerlach/Visuals Unlimited, p. 11 (top); © Kjell B. Sandved/Visuals Unlimited, p. 11 (right); © James Urbach/SuperStock, p. 12; © Hans Christoph Kappel/naturepl.com, pp. 14, 15 (right); © Dick Poe/Visuals Unlimited, p. 15 (left); © Wally Eberhart/Visuals Unlimited, p. 16; © Bob Wilson/Visuals Unlimited, p. 18 (right); © Jeff Milton/Daybreak Imagery, p. 19 (right); © Rolf Nussbaumer/naturepl.com, p. 20 (top); © Stephen Dalton/Minden Pictures, p. 22; © Bernard Castelein/naturepl.com, p. 23; © Carlos Adolfo Sastoque N./SuperStock, p. 24; © Satoshi Kuribayashi/Oxford Scientific Films, p. 25; © Kenneth H. Thomas/Photo Researchers, Inc., p. 26 (top); © Leroy Simon/Visuals Unlimited, pp. 26 (bottom), 30, 34 (right); © Christopher Hunt/Getty Images, p. 27 (top); © Piotr Naskrecki/Minden Pictures, p. 27 (bottom); © Michael P. Gadomski/SuperStock, p. 28 (left); © Gary Vestal/Photographer's Choice/Getty Images, p. 28 (right); © Laura Westlund/Independent Picture Service, p. 29; © Siegel, R./Peter Arnold, Inc., p. 31; © Ray Coleman/Visuals Unlimited, p. 32; © M. Fogden/OSF/Animals Animals-Earth Scenes, p. 35 (left); © First Light/Pierre Desrosiers/Getty Images, p. 37; © Ross Frid/Visuals Unlimited, p. 38 (top); © Aurora/James Balog/Getty Images, p. 39; © Fritz Polking/Visuals Unlimited, p. 40; © Frans Lanting/Minden Pictures, p. 41; © Ken Lucas/Visuals Unlimited, p. 42; © Peter Mason/Taxi/Getty Images, p. 43.

Front cover: © Richard Day/Daybreak Imagery
Back cover: PhotoDisc Royalty Free by Getty Images